great cui

WEEKLY

thai
cooking

In the *Great Cuisines* cookbook series you'll be introduced to the food of some of the great cooking nations of the world. The recipes contain readily available ingredients and use familiar cooking techniques so you can recreate the world's most delectable meals with the greatest of ease.

All recipes serve 4 unless stated otherwise.

Pamela Clark

Food Editor

Coriander is a bright-green leafy herb with a pungent flavour. Also known as cilantro or Chinese parsley, the roots of coriander are also used in cooking – often to contribute flavour to a curry paste without adding a green hue (as would the leaves).

coriander

Chillies are part of the *capsicum* family, and are available in many varieties and forms. Generally, the smaller a chilli is (eg. a birdseye chilli), the more it packs a punch heat-wise. Removing membranes and seeds from fresh chillies will help reduce the heat level. It is a good idea to wear kitchen gloves when seeding and chopping chillies, as they can burn your skin. Dried, powdered and flaked chillies are widely available, as is sambal oelek, an Indonesian chilli paste. Thai chillies range in colour from bright-red to dark-green, and are medium-hot to taste.

Kaffir limes are a medium-sized citrus fruit with a thick, wrinkly, dark-green skin. The fragrant leaves of the same tree and the rind of the fruit lend a distinctive, aromatic flavour to soups, salads and curries, and are commonly used in Thai cooking. Kaffir lime leaves are available fresh or dried.

kaffir limes

sambal oelek

birdseye chillies

Thai chillies

dried chilli flakes

dried chillies

chilli powder

4 prawns with

lemon grass and mint

750g medium
uncooked prawns

2 tablespoons
chopped fresh
mint leaves

2 tablespoons finely
chopped fresh
lemon grass

2 cloves garlic,
crushed

1 teaspoon finely
grated lemon rind

2 tablespoons
lemon juice

2 teaspoons
sambal oelek

1/4 cup (60ml)
peanut oil

1 medium
carrot (120g)

100g snow
peas, sliced

1 tablespoon
brown vinegar

1 teaspoon
brown sugar

1 teaspoon soy sauce

Shell and devein prawns, leaving tails intact. Combine prawns in large bowl with mint, lemon grass, garlic, rind, juice and sambal, cover; refrigerate 10 minutes.

Heat 1 tablespoon of the oil in wok or large frying pan; stir-fry prawn mixture, in batches, until prawns are changed in colour. Using vegetable peeler, slice carrot into thin ribbons. Add snow peas and carrot strips to same wok; stir-fry, tossing until just tender.

Return prawn mixture to wok; stir-fry, tossing with vegetables until combined. To serve, drizzle combined remaining oil, vinegar, sugar and soy sauce over prawn mixture.

6 fried noodles with
pork and peanuts

500g Hokkien noodles

2 teaspoons red curry paste (see page 32)

400g pork fillets, sliced thinly

1 tablespoon peanut oil

1 chicken stock cube

1 tablespoon soy sauce

2 teaspoons fish sauce

2 teaspoons cornflour

1/2 cup (125ml) water

1/3 cup (50g) unsalted roasted peanuts

2 tablespoons chopped fresh coriander leaves

Rinse noodles under hot water; drain. Transfer to large bowl; separate with fork.

Rub curry paste over pork. Heat 1/2 of the oil in wok or large frying pan; stir-fry pork, in batches, until browned all over and cooked as desired.

Heat remaining oil in same wok, add noodles; stir-fry, tossing until hot. Add crumbled stock cube, sauces and blended cornflour and water; stir-fry until mixture boils and thickens slightly. Return pork to pan with peanuts and coriander; stir-fry, tossing until hot.

massaman

beef curry

1kg topside steak

¹/₄ cup (60ml)
vegetable oil

500g small
potatoes, halved

250g small
onions, halved

¹/₃ cup massaman
curry paste (see
page 33)

2 x 340ml cans
coconut cream

1 teaspoon tamarind
concentrate

²/₃ cup (160ml)
hot water

¹/₄ cup (50g)
brown sugar

Cut steak into 3cm cubes. Heat oil in large saucepan; add steak,
in batches, stir over high heat until steak is browned all over.
Remove steak from pan, drain on absorbent paper.
Add potato and onion to same pan, stir over high heat until lightly
browned. Stir in curry paste, stir over heat further 1 minute.
Stir in coconut cream, then steak, combined tamarind concentrate,
water and sugar; bring to a boil. Reduce heat; simmer, uncovered,
about 45 minutes or until meat is tender and mixture has thickened.

Serves 6

8 lamb satay

Soak bamboo skewers in water for about 1 hour to prevent them scorching.

1kg lamb round roast

2 teaspoons peanut oil

1 tablespoon finely chopped fresh lemon grass

2 teaspoons ground cumin

1½ cups (375ml) chicken stock

½ cup (130g) smooth peanut butter

¼ cup (60ml) sweet chilli sauce

2 teaspoons lemon juice

1 tablespoon finely chopped fresh coriander leaves

Cut lamb into 3cm pieces; thread onto 12 skewers.
Heat oil in medium saucepan; cook lemon grass and cumin, stirring, until fragrant. Add remaining ingredients, bring to a boil, stirring; simmer, uncovered, 5 minutes.
Cook skewers, in batches, in heated oiled grill pan (or on barbecue) until browned all over and cooked as desired; serve skewers with hot satay sauce.

thai **beef** salad 9

500g beef rump steak

*2 Lebanese
cucumbers (260g)*

*5 large egg
tomatoes (450g)*

*2 cups (160g)
bean sprouts*

*1 tablespoon small
fresh mint leaves*

thai dressing

*1/4 cup (60ml) sweet
chilli sauce*

*1 tablespoon
fish sauce*

*1 tablespoon
lime juice*

1 clove garlic, crushed

*2 tablespoons
chopped fresh
coriander leaves*

*1 tablespoon chopped
fresh mint leaves*

Brush beef with 1/4 cup (60ml) of the Thai Dressing. Cook beef in
heated oiled grill pan (or on barbecue) until browned both sides and
cooked as desired. Remove from heat, cover; stand for 10 minutes
before slicing thinly.

Meanwhile, halve cucumbers lengthways, scoop out and discard
seeds; slice thinly. Cut tomatoes in quarters lengthways, remove and
discard seeds; slice thinly. Just before serving, toss beef in medium
bowl with cucumber, tomato, sprouts and remaining Dressing; sprinkle
with mint leaves.

Thai Dressing Combine ingredients in jar; shake well.

10 red curry, coconut
and lamb stir-fry

2 tablespoons
peanut oil

500g lamb strips

1 large white onion
(200g), sliced

1 tablespoon red curry
paste (see page 32)

1 tablespoon finely
chopped fresh
lemon grass

2 cloves garlic,
crushed

1 tablespoon
fish sauce

100g snake
beans, chopped

500g choy sum,
trimmed

1 cup (250ml)
coconut cream

1/4 cup finely chopped
fresh coriander leaves

Heat half of the oil in wok or large frying pan; stir-fry lamb, in batches, until browned and almost cooked through. Heat remaining oil in same wok; stir-fry onion, paste, lemon grass, garlic and sauce until onion is just soft.
Add beans and choy sum; stir-fry until vegetables are just tender. Return lamb to pan with cream and coriander; stir-fry, tossing until hot.

12 stir-fried steak
with green beans

2 tablespoons vegetable oil

1 medium brown onion
(150g), chopped finely

2 cloves garlic, crushed

1 large fresh green chilli,
chopped finely

1 large fresh red chilli,
chopped finely

180g green beans, halved

500g beef rump steak, sliced thinly

1 tablespoon fish sauce

1 tablespoon finely chopped
fresh coriander leaves

1 teaspoon sugar

Heat 1/2 the oil in wok or large frying pan; stir-fry onion, garlic, chillies and beans until beans are just tender, remove from wok. Heat remaining oil in same wok; stir-fry beef until just cooked. **Return** bean mixture to wok with sauce, coriander and sugar; stir-fry, tossing until hot.

gingered beef

and coconut soup

500g Hokkien noodles

750g beef rump steak, sliced thinly

1/4 cup (70g) red curry paste (see page 32)

1 tablespoon finely chopped fresh lemon grass

1/3 cup (80ml) lime juice

1 tablespoon peanut oil

1 tablespoon grated fresh ginger

1 litre (4 cups) beef stock

800ml coconut milk

1 tablespoon brown sugar

1 tablespoon fish sauce

425g can straw mushrooms, rinsed, drained, halved

1/4 cup finely chopped fresh coriander leaves

1/4 cup loosely packed fresh mint leaves

100g watercress sprigs

Rinse noodles under hot water; drain. Transfer to large bowl; separate with fork.

Combine beef with 1 tablespoon of the curry paste, lemon grass and 1 tablespoon of the juice in large bowl. Cover; refrigerate 10 minutes.

Heat oil in large saucepan; cook beef mixture, in batches, until browned all over and almost cooked. Add remaining curry paste and ginger to same pan; cook, stirring, until fragrant. Add remaining juice, stock, milk, sugar and sauce; simmer, covered, 20 minutes. Stir in noodles, beef, mushrooms and coriander; simmer, uncovered, until hot. Serve sprinkled with mint and watercress.

2 tablespoons peanut oil

1kg pumpkin, chopped coarsely

1 medium carrot (120g), chopped coarsely

1 medium potato (200g), chopped coarsely

1 medium brown onion (150g), chopped coarsely

1 litre (4 cups) chicken stock

3 teaspoons sambal oelek

1 tablespoon finely chopped fresh lemon grass

3 teaspoons lime juice

1½ teaspoons garam masala

75g bean thread vermicelli noodles

¾ cup (180ml) coconut milk

¼ cup (15g) shredded coconut, toasted

2 tablespoons fresh coriander leaves

Heat oil in large saucepan; cook pumpkin, carrot, potato and onion, stirring, until browned lightly. Stir in stock, sambal, lemon grass, juice and garam masala. Bring to a boil; simmer, uncovered, 30 minutes.

Meanwhile, cut noodles into 5cm lengths, place in medium heatproof bowl, cover with boiling water, stand only until just tender; drain.

Blend or process pumpkin mixture, in batches, until smooth; return to pan. Stir in milk and noodles. Bring to a boil; simmer, stirring, 2 minutes.

Ladle hot soup into serving bowls; sprinkle with coconut and coriander.

coconut beef soup

500g beef strips

1/4 cup green curry paste (see page 32)

2 tablespoons finely chopped fresh lemon grass

1 tablespoon finely grated lime rind

1/3 cup (80ml) lime juice

1 tablespoon vegetable oil

3 cloves garlic, crushed

1 litre (4 cups) beef stock

800ml coconut milk

1 tablespoon brown sugar

1 tablespoon fish sauce

425g can straw mushrooms, rinsed, drained

100g bean thread vermicelli noodles

Combine beef in medium bowl with 1 tablespoon of the paste, lemon grass, rind and 1 tablespoon of the juice. Cover; refrigerate 10 minutes.
Heat oil in large saucepan; cook beef mixture, in batches, until browned all over. Cook remaining paste and garlic in same pan until fragrant. Add remaining juice, stock, milk, sugar and sauce; simmer, uncovered, 30 minutes.
Return beef and any juices to pan with mushrooms and noodles; simmer, uncovered, about 5 minutes or until noodles are tender. Serve soup sprinkled with flaked toasted coconut and fresh coriander leaves, if desired.

thai-style

chicken soup

1 tablespoon peanut oil

1 medium leek (350g),
sliced finely

1 clove garlic, crushed

1 teaspoon mild
curry powder

1 teaspoon ground cumin

1/2 teaspoon
ground coriander

500g chicken thigh fillets,
sliced thinly

1 litre (4 cups)
chicken stock

1 stem fresh lemon
grass, halved

1²/₃ cups (400ml)
coconut milk

2 teaspoons
sambal oelek

1 tablespoon cornflour

1 tablespoon water, extra

1 teaspoon fish sauce

1 small red capsicum
(150g), sliced

4 green onions,
chopped finely

1 tablespoon lime juice

1 tablespoon finely
chopped fresh
coriander leaves

Heat oil in large saucepan; cook leek and
garlic until leek is soft. Add curry powder,
cumin and ground coriander; cook, stirring,
until fragrant. Add chicken; cook, stirring,
until chicken is browned lightly.

Stir in stock, lemon grass, milk and
sambal. Bring to a boil; simmer, uncovered,
10 minutes. Stir in blended cornflour and
extra water, and fish sauce; stir over heat
until soup boils and thickens slightly.

Just before serving, remove and discard
lemon grass. Stir in capsicum, onion, juice
and fresh coriander.

thai-style
noodle soup

2 tablespoons
vegetable oil

2 medium brown onions
(300g), chopped

2 cloves garlic, crushed

2 stems fresh lemon
grass, chopped finely

1/2 teaspoon
sambal oelek

2 teaspoons
ground turmeric

2 teaspoons
ground ginger

1 litre (4 cups)
chicken stock

2 tablespoons lime juice

2 cups (500ml)
coconut milk

2 cups (340g) chopped
cooked chicken

1 1/2 cups (120g) finely
shredded cabbage

1/2 medium red capsicum
(100g), sliced thinly

4 green onions,
chopped finely

200g thin dried
wheat noodles

1 1/4 cups (100g)
bean sprouts

Heat oil in large saucepan; cook brown
onion, garlic and lemon grass, stirring,
until onion is soft.

Stir in sambal, turmeric and ginger; cook
until fragrant. Add stock and juice; simmer,
covered, 10 minutes. Add milk, chicken,
cabbage, capsicum, green onion and
noodles; simmer, uncovered, about
5 minutes or until noodles are tender.
Stir in bean sprouts.

18 baked garlic
quail

4 quail

4 cloves garlic, crushed

¼ cup (60ml) sambal oelek

2 tablespoons honey

2 tablespoons soy sauce

2 teaspoons brown sugar

2 tablespoons vegetable oil

Cut quail in half lengthways.
Combine garlic, sambal, honey,
sauce, sugar and oil in large
bowl, add quail; mix well.
Cover, refrigerate 10 minutes.
Drain quail over medium bowl;
reserve marinade. Place quail
on wire rack over baking
dish; brush with reserved
marinade. Bake, uncovered,
in moderate oven 15 minutes,
increase temperature to hot;
bake about 10 minutes or
until quail are crisp and
cooked through.

chilli and lemon grass
spatchcocks

2 tablespoons
sambal oelek

1 tablespoon coarsely
chopped fresh
lemon grass

3/4 cup (180ml)
coconut milk

1 tablespoon coarsely
chopped fresh
coriander leaves

2 teaspoons grated
fresh ginger

2 cloves garlic,
quartered

1/2 teaspoon
ground turmeric

4 x 500g spatchcocks,
halved

Blend or process sambal, lemon grass, milk, coriander, ginger, garlic
and turmeric until almost smooth. Pour mixture over spatchcocks in
shallow dish. Cover; refrigerate 3 hours or overnight.
Drain spatchcocks over medium bowl; reserve marinade. Char-grill
(or barbecue) spatchcocks until browned both sides and cooked
through, brushing with reserved marinade during cooking.

with sweet vinegar sauce

1kg chicken thigh fillets, halved

1/2 cup (125ml) coconut milk

paste

4 cloves garlic, crushed

1 teaspoon cracked black pepper

2 teaspoons sugar

1 tablespoon sweet paprika

1 tablespoon coarsely chopped fresh coriander root

1 teaspoon mild curry powder

2 birdseye chillies, quartered

1 tablespoon vegetable oil

sweet vinegar sauce

1 birdseye chilli, quartered

2 cloves garlic, crushed

1/2 cup (125ml) white vinegar

2 tablespoons raw sugar

Combine chicken with Paste in large bowl. Cover; refrigerate 15 minutes. Grill chicken until browned on both sides and cooked through, basting with milk several times during cooking. Serve with Sweet Vinegar Sauce.
Paste Grind ingredients to a paste, using a mortar and pestle.
Sweet Vinegar Sauce Grind chilli and garlic to a paste using a mortar and pestle. Combine vinegar and sugar in small saucepan, stir over heat, without boiling, until sugar is dissolved. Bring to a boil; simmer, uncovered, without stirring, until syrup just begins to colour. Remove from heat, cool slightly; stir in chilli paste.

22 sweet and sour
pork spare ribs

1 tablespoon
vegetable oil

2 cloves garlic,
crushed

1/2 medium red onion
(85g), chopped

2 tablespoons sugar

2 tablespoons
lime juice

1/4 cup (60ml)
sweetened
pineapple juice

2 teaspoons
fish sauce

1 tablespoon
oyster sauce

1/3 cup (80ml)
tomato sauce

1 tablespoon sweet
chilli sauce

1 tablespoon
white vinegar

1kg pork spare ribs

Heat oil in small saucepan; cook garlic and onion, stirring, until onion
is soft. Stir in sugar, juices, sauces and vinegar; bring to a boil. Simmer,
uncovered, about 2 minutes or until thickened slightly.

Place spare ribs on wire rack over baking dish, brush with sweet
and sour sauce. Bake, uncovered, in hot oven 10 minutes, reduce
heat to moderate; bake about 15 minutes or until pork is crisp and
cooked through. Turn and baste ribs several times during cooking.

thai-style lamb
patties with chilli sauce

1 tablespoon
vegetable oil

2 green onions,
chopped finely

2 tablespoons red curry
paste (see page 32)

1 clove garlic, crushed

500g minced lamb

1 cup (70g) stale
breadcrumbs

2 tablespoons chopped
fresh coriander leaves

¼ cup (60ml)
coconut milk

1 teaspoon finely
grated lime rind

vegetable oil, for
shallow-frying

chilli sauce

1 tablespoon water

1 tablespoon
white vinegar

1 tablespoon sweet
chilli sauce

1 tablespoon finely
chopped unsalted
roasted peanuts

2 teaspoons soy sauce

1 teaspoon sugar

Heat oil in small saucepan; cook onion,
paste and garlic, stirring, until fragrant, cool.
Combine mince in medium bowl with onion
mixture, breadcrumbs, coriander, milk
and rind; mix well.

Using damp hands, shape mixture into
8 patties; refrigerate until firm. Shallow-fry
patties, in hot oil, in large frying pan,
until browned both sides and cooked
through; drain on absorbent paper.
Serve with Chilli sauce.

Chilli Sauce Combine ingredients in small
pan, stir over heat until sugar is dissolved.

sweet chilli chicken
with cashews

700g single chicken
breast fillets,
sliced thinly

1/4 cup finely chopped
fresh coriander leaves

2 birdseye chillies,
seeded, chopped
finely

1 tablespoon
sesame oil

1 clove garlic, crushed

2 tablespoons
peanut oil

1/3 cup (80ml)
rice vinegar

1/4 cup (60ml) sweet
chilli sauce

1 tablespoon
lime juice

3/4 cup (110g) raw
cashews, toasted

1 cup (55g) snow
pea sprouts

Combine chicken, coriander, chilli, sesame oil and garlic in large bowl.
Cover; refrigerate 3 hours or overnight.

Heat peanut oil in wok or large frying pan; stir-fry chicken mixture, in
batches, until chicken is browned and cooked through.

Return chicken mixture to wok with vinegar, sauce and juice; stir-fry until
sauce boils. Add cashews; stir-fry, tossing, until combined. Remove wok
from heat, gently toss sprouts with chicken mixture.

peppered prawns 25
with leek

1 medium leek (350g)

*500g large
uncooked prawns*

*2 tablespoons
vegetable oil*

1 clove garlic, crushed

1 tablespoon fish sauce

1 teaspoon brown sugar

*1 teaspoon cracked
black pepper*

*2 teaspoons finely chopped
fresh coriander leaves*

Cut leek into 3cm pieces.
Cook leek in large pan of
boiling water, uncovered,
until just tender; drain.
Shell prawns, leaving
tails intact. Cut along
centre back of prawns,
remove vein, flatten
prawns slightly.
Heat oil in wok or large
frying pan; stir-fry prawns
and garlic for 2 minutes.
Add sauce, sugar and
pepper; stir-fry until prawns
are changed in colour.
Serve prawns over leek,
pour over cooking liquid;
sprinkle with coriander.
Serves 2

26 fish with sweet
and sour vegetables

1.5kg whole white fish

2 tablespoons fish sauce

1 tablespoon vegetable oil

1 medium lime (80g), sliced

3 green onions,
chopped finely

2 tablespoons chopped
fresh coriander leaves

**sweet and sour
vegetables**

10 dried shiitake
mushrooms (20g)

1 tablespoon vegetable oil

2 cloves garlic, crushed

1 tablespoon grated
fresh ginger

2 tablespoons brown sugar

2 tablespoons white vinegar

2 tablespoons fish sauce

1 medium tomato (190g),
peeled, seeded, chopped

1 medium yellow capsicum
(200g), chopped coarsely

1 medium red capsicum
(200g), chopped coarsely

10 baby carrots
(200g), chopped

1/4 cup (60ml) water

Score fish with 4 cuts on each side, pour fish sauce into slits.

Heat oil in flameproof baking dish, add fish; cook over high heat on both sides to seal. Transfer dish to oven; bake, covered, in hot oven about 30 minutes or until fish is cooked through.

Serve with Sweet and Sour Vegetables and lime slices; sprinkle with green onion and coriander leaves.

Sweet and Sour Vegetables
Place mushrooms in small heatproof bowl, cover with boiling water, stand 20 minutes; drain. Discard stems, halve caps.

Heat oil in wok or large frying pan; stir-fry garlic and ginger until fragrant. Add sugar, vinegar and sauce; cook, stirring, until sugar is dissolved. Stir in mushrooms and remaining ingredients; simmer, covered, about 3 minutes or until vegetables are just tender.

28 aromatic chicken
with thai eggplant

2 cups coarsely
chopped fresh
coriander leaves

2 tablespoons finely
chopped fresh
lemon grass

1 tablespoon finely
grated lime rind

2 tablespoons
lime juice

2 tablespoons grated
fresh ginger

1 tablespoon
ground turmeric

1 tablespoon
ground coriander

1 tablespoon
ground cumin

1/3 cup (80ml)
peanut oil

700g single chicken
breast fillets,
sliced thinly

250g Thai eggplants

1 medium brown onion
(150g), sliced finely

3 cups (240g)
bean sprouts

Blend or process fresh coriander, lemon grass, rind, juice, ginger, turmeric, ground coriander and cumin with 1/2 of the oil until the mixture forms a paste.

Combine chicken in large bowl with coriander paste; mix well.

Discard stems from eggplants; stir-fry eggplants in dry heated wok or large frying pan for 2 minutes, remove from wok. Heat remaining oil in same wok; stir-fry chicken mixture and onion, in batches, until chicken is cooked through.

Return chicken to wok with eggplants and sprouts; stir-fry, tossing until sprouts are just wilted.

hot and sour
prawn soup (tom yum goong)

800g large
uncooked prawns

1 tablespoon
peanut oil

3 cloves garlic, halved

2 birdseye chillies,
halved

2 stems fresh lemon
grass, quartered

6 fresh kaffir
lime leaves,
chopped roughly

2 litres (8 cups) water

1/3 cup (80ml)
lemon juice

2 teaspoons
brown sugar

2 tablespoons
fish sauce

2 fresh coriander roots

1/4 cup finely chopped
fresh coriander leaves

2 green onions,
chopped finely

Shell and devein prawns, leaving tails intact.
Discard heads; reserve shells. Heat oil in large
saucepan, add prawn shells, garlic and chilli;
cook, stirring, about 5 minutes or until shells
are red and mixture is fragrant. Add lemon
grass, lime leaves, water, juice, sugar, sauce
and coriander roots. Bring to a boil; simmer,
covered, 30 minutes.

Strain stock; reserve lime leaves. Place strained
stock, reserved lime leaves, prawns, coriander
leaves and onion into clean pan. Bring to a
boil; simmer, covered, about 3 minutes or until
prawns are changed in colour.

30 chilli **chicken** with
basil and coconut cream

2 tablespoons
vegetable oil

1 medium brown
onion (150g),
chopped finely

2 tablespoons
finely chopped
birdseye chillies

500g single chicken
breast fillets,
sliced thickly

1 cup finely shredded
fresh basil leaves

2 tablespoons
fish sauce

1 teaspoon finely
chopped fresh
coriander root

1¹/₂ teaspoons sugar

1 cup (250ml)
coconut cream

Heat oil in wok or large frying pan; stir-fry onion and chilli until onion
is soft. Add chicken; stir-fry until chicken is cooked through. Add
basil, sauce, coriander root and sugar; stir-fry, tossing, 1 minute.
Add cream; stir-fry, tossing until hot.

thai salad with

crunchy rice squares

300g bok choy, chopped

1 medium yellow capsicum (200g), sliced

1 medium red capsicum (200g), sliced finely

1¼ cups (125g) mung bean sprouts

2 cups (160g) bean sprouts

2 tablespoons shredded fresh basil leaves

coconut cream dressing

½ cup (125ml) coconut cream

2 tablespoons lime juice

½ teaspoon sesame oil

½ teaspoon honey

½ teaspoon fish sauce

rice squares

1 cup (200g) white short-grain rice

2 cups (500ml) chicken stock

1 tablespoon chopped fresh basil leaves

½ teaspoon sambal oelek

vegetable oil, for deep-frying

Combine bok choy, capsicum, sprouts and basil in large bowl, add Coconut Cream Dressing; mix well. Top with Rice Squares.

Coconut Cream Dressing Combine ingredients in jar; shake well.

Rice Squares Grease deep 15cm square cake pan, line base and sides with baking paper. Combine rice and stock in medium saucepan, bring to a boil; simmer, covered with tight-fitting lid, about 12 minutes or until rice is tender and sticky and liquid absorbed. Stir in basil and sambal. Press mixture firmly into prepared pan, smooth top. Cover with baking paper, place another pan on top; weigh down with heavy cans. Refrigerate 3 hours or overnight. Remove rice mixture from pan, cut into 2cm squares. Heat vegetable oil in large saucepan; deep-fry rice squares, in batches, until browned and crisp. Drain rice squares on absorbent paper.

32 curry pastes

Red and green curry pastes are used in chicken, seafood and beef curries. Massaman curry paste is traditionally used in a meat and potato curry. Store pastes in an airtight container in the refrigerator for up to 3 weeks.

red curry paste

1 small red onion (100g), chopped coarsely

3 cloves garlic, halved

2 tablespoons coarsely chopped fresh lemon grass

3 teaspoons chopped fresh coriander root

2 teaspoons dried chilli flakes

1 teaspoon galangal powder

1 teaspoon finely grated lime rind

1/2 teaspoon shrimp paste

1 dried kaffir lime leaf

3 teaspoons hot paprika

1/2 teaspoon ground turmeric

1/2 teaspoon cumin seeds

3 teaspoons peanut oil

Blend or process ingredients until smooth.

Makes about 1/4 cup

green curry paste

3 small fresh chillies, seeded, sliced thickly

3 green onions, chopped coarsely

2 cloves garlic, halved

1/4 cup coarsely chopped fresh coriander leaves

1/4 cup coarsely chopped fresh lemon grass

1/4 cup (60ml) peanut oil

2 tablespoons water

1 teaspoon shrimp paste

1/2 teaspoon ground cumin

225g can bamboo shoots, drained, sliced thickly

Blend or process ingredients until smooth.

Makes about 3/4 cup

opposite, from top: massaman curry paste; green curry paste; and red curry paste.

massaman curry paste

4 small fresh red chillies,
seeded, halved

4 cloves garlic, halved

3 green onions,
chopped coarsely

2 teaspoons coarsely chopped
fresh lemon grass

2 teaspoons peanut oil

2 teaspoons sugar

$1/2$ teaspoon ground cumin

$1/2$ teaspoon ground cardamom

$1/4$ teaspoon ground cinnamon

$1/4$ teaspoon ground cloves

$1/4$ teaspoon ground turmeric

2 tablespoons water

Blend or process ingredients
until combined. Add a little
extra water, if necessary, to
make a paste.

Makes about $1/3$ cup

34 fish balls

750g firm white fish fillets

2 tablespoons fish sauce

2 cloves garlic, crushed

1 tablespoon finely grated fresh ginger

1/4 cup (70g) green curry paste
(see page 32)

2 tablespoons lime juice

1/3 cup finely chopped fresh coriander leaves

1 egg

1 1/2 cups (375ml) vegetable stock

1 cup (250ml) coconut milk

Cut fish into 3cm pieces; blend or process fish pieces with sauce, garlic, ginger, 2 tablespoons of the paste, 2 teaspoons of the juice, 1/2 the coriander and egg until a smooth paste forms.
Roll level tablespoons of mixture into balls; place in single layer on tray. Cover; refrigerate 30 minutes.
Bring stock to a boil in large saucepan. Add fish balls; simmer, covered, about 5 minutes or until cooked through, stirring occasionally to gently turn fish balls in stock. Remove fish balls from stock; cover to keep warm. Discard stock.
Cook remaining curry paste in same pan, stirring, until fragrant. Add milk; cook, stirring, until mixture boils. Add fish balls and remaining juice and coriander; stir until heated through.

36 thai green
fish curry

2 tablespoons
peanut oil

750g piece fresh tuna,
chopped coarsely

2 medium white
onions (300g),
chopped coarsely

2 cloves garlic,
crushed

1 tablespoon finely
chopped fresh
lemon grass

1 tablespoon grated
fresh ginger

2 tablespoons
green curry paste
(see page 32)

1^2/$_3$ cups (400ml)
coconut cream

2 tablespoons
lime juice

1 tablespoon thick
tamarind concentrate

1 tablespoon coarsely
chopped fresh
coriander leaves

1 cup (80g)
bean sprouts

250g snow peas, sliced

Heat 1/2 of the oil in large frying pan; cook fish,
in batches, until just browned. Heat remaining
oil in same pan; cook onion, garlic, lemon grass
and ginger, stirring, until onion is soft. Add
paste; cook, stirring, until fragrant.
Return fish to pan with remaining ingredients;
cook, stirring gently, until sprouts are just wilted.

pork and
baby corn stir-fry

2 teaspoons
peanut oil

750g pork strips

1/4 cup green curry
paste (see page 32)

100g fresh baby
corn, halved

1 large red capsicum
(350g), sliced thinly

2/3 cup (160ml)
coconut milk

1 1/2 tablespoons
lime juice

200g baby
spinach leaves

1/3 cup coarsely
shredded fresh
basil leaves

Heat oil in wok or large frying pan; stir-fry pork, in batches, until browned
all over and cooked through. Add paste to same wok; stir-fry until fragrant.
Add corn and capsicum; stir-fry 2 minutes. Add milk and juice; stir-fry
2 minutes. Return pork to wok with spinach and basil; stir-fry, tossing
until leaves are just wilted.

38 chicken noodle
stir-fry

180g dried rice noodles

700g single chicken breast fillets, sliced thinly

2 teaspoons grated fresh ginger

2 tablespoons peanut oil

4 green onions, sliced finely

1½ cups (120g) bean sprouts

2 (300g) baby bok choy, chopped coarsely

⅓ cup (80ml) lime juice

¼ cup (60ml) sweet chilli sauce

2 teaspoons fish sauce

1½ tablespoons sugar

2 tablespoons finely chopped fresh
coriander leaves

1 tablespoon finely chopped fresh mint leaves

Place noodles in large heatproof bowl, cover
with boiling water, stand only until just tender;
drain. Cover to keep warm.
Combine chicken and ginger in medium bowl.
Heat oil in wok or large frying pan; stir-fry
chicken, in batches, until browned all over.
Return chicken to wok with onion, sprouts,
bok choy and remaining ingredients; stir-fry,
tossing until hot. Serve chicken mixture over
rice noodles.

40 chilli prawns
and noodles

1kg large
cooked prawns

250g rice
vermicelli noodles

4 green onions,
sliced finely

1 large red capsicum
(350g), sliced finely

2 cups (160g)
bean sprouts

1/2 cup (75g) coarsely
chopped unsalted
roasted peanuts

1 tablespoon coarsely
chopped fresh
coriander leaves

chilli dressing

2 tablespoons
peanut oil

1/4 cup (60ml)
soy sauce

1 tablespoon
lime juice

2 teaspoons
brown sugar

1 teaspoon
tomato sauce

1 birdseye chilli,
seeded, chopped
finely

Shell and devein prawns, leaving tails intact.
Place noodles in medium heatproof bowl,
cover with boiling water, stand only until just
tender; drain. Combine prawns, noodles,
remaining ingredients and Chilli Dressing
in large bowl; mix gently.
Chilli Dressing Combine ingredients in jar;
shake well.

snapper filled with thai-style vegetables

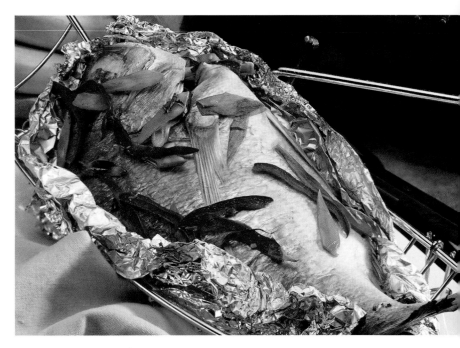

2 medium red capsicums (400g), sliced thinly

6 green onions, sliced thinly

200g snow peas, sliced thinly

2 tablespoons thinly sliced fresh ginger

2 tablespoons sweet chilli sauce

2 teaspoons fish sauce

2 tablespoons lime juice

1/3 cup fresh basil leaves

1/2 cup fresh coriander leaves

1.5kg whole snapper

Combine capsicum, onion, snow peas, ginger, sauces, juice and herbs in medium bowl. Fill fish cavity with vegetable mixture. Wrap fish in oiled foil, place in baking dish. **Bake** in hot oven about 30 minutes or until fish is just cooked through.

Cook chicken in heated oiled grill pan (or on barbecue) until browned both sides and tender. Remove from pan; cut into 1cm slices. Halve the cucumber lengthways; discard seeds, cut into 1cm slices. Cut asparagus into 3cm lengths; boil, steam or microwave until just tender. Rinse under cold water; drain.

Place noodles in large heatproof bowl, cover with boiling water, stand until just tender. Rinse under cold water; drain.

Combine chicken and noodles in large bowl with cucumber, asparagus, onion, capsicum, sprouts, peanuts and herbs. Just before serving, gently toss in remaining ingredients.

700g single chicken breast fillets

1 large green cucumber (400g)

250g asparagus

150g dried rice noodles

3 green onions, sliced finely

1 medium red capsicum (200g), sliced finely

1 cup (80g) bean sprouts

1/3 cup (50g) unsalted roasted peanuts, chopped coarsely

1/4 cup finely chopped fresh mint leaves

2 tablespoons chopped fresh coriander leaves

1/3 cup (80ml) lime juice

1/4 cup (60ml) vegetable oil

2 tablespoons finely chopped fresh lemon grass

3 birdseye chillies, seeded, sliced thinly

1 1/2 tablespoons fish sauce

2 teaspoons brown sugar

1 clove garlic, crushed

pork, prawn and

noodle stir-fry (pad thai)

*375g dried
rice noodles*

*¹/₄ cup (65g)
palm sugar*

2 teaspoons soy sauce

*1 tablespoon
tomato sauce*

*¹/₄ cup (60ml) mild
chilli sauce*

*¹/₄ cup (60ml)
fish sauce*

*1 tablespoon
peanut oil*

200g minced pork

2 cloves garlic, crushed

*1 tablespoon grated
fresh ginger*

3 eggs, beaten lightly

*200g medium cooked
prawns, shelled*

*1 birdseye chilli,
chopped finely*

2 green onions, sliced

*2 cups (160g)
bean sprouts*

*2 tablespoons chopped
fresh coriander leaves*

*¹/₂ cup (75g) unsalted
roasted peanuts,
chopped coarsely*

Place noodles in large heatproof bowl, cover with boiling water, stand until just tender; drain.
Combine sugar and sauces in small saucepan; cook, stirring, until sugar dissolves.
Heat oil in wok or large frying pan; stir-fry pork, garlic and ginger until pork is browned and almost cooked. Add eggs and prawns; gently stir-fry, until egg sets. Add noodles, sauce mixture and remaining ingredients; gently stir-fry until heated through. If desired, serve with fresh lime wedges.

44 squid with
red and green capsicums

500g squid hoods

1 large green capsicum (350g)

1 large red capsicum (350g)

1 tablespoon vegetable oil

4 cloves garlic, sliced

1/3 cup (80ml) water

1 tablespoon palm sugar

1 tablespoon fish sauce

1 tablespoon sweet chilli sauce

Cut squid hoods in half; score shallow criss-cross pattern on inside surface, cut into 2cm x 3cm pieces.

Quarter capsicums, remove seeds and membranes. Grill capsicums, skin-side up, until skin blisters and blackens. Peel away skin; cut capsicum the same size as squid.

Heat oil in wok or large frying pan; stir-fry garlic until fragrant. Add squid, water, sugar and fish sauce; stir-fry until squid curls. Add capsicum and chilli sauce; stir-fry, tossing until hot.

sweet and sour tofu

375g firm tofu

¼ cup (60ml) vegetable oil

1 clove garlic, sliced

200g green beans, sliced

1 medium brown onion
(150g), sliced coarsely

1 medium carrot (120g),
sliced finely

200g broccoli, cut into florets

1 trimmed (75g) celery stick, sliced

2 green onions, chopped

1 tablespoon tamarind sauce

1 tablespoon fish sauce

2 tablespoons oyster sauce

1 tablespoon soy sauce

1 tablespoon sweet chilli sauce

1 tablespoon tomato paste

2 tablespoons sugar

1 tablespoon white vinegar

¼ teaspoon ground star anise

1 teaspoon cornflour

1 cup (250ml) water

Cut tofu into 1.5cm cubes. Heat oil in large frying pan; cook garlic,
stirring, 30 seconds, remove and discard garlic. Cook tofu, in batches,
in same pan, until browned lightly; remove from pan.
Cook beans, brown onion and carrot in same pan, stirring, until vegetables
are almost tender. Add broccoli, celery, green onion, sauces, paste,
sugar, vinegar and star anise; cook for 2 minutes. Stir in tofu with
blended cornflour and water; stir gently until sauce boils and thickens.

seafood salad

500g squid hoods

500g medium
cooked prawns

1/2 cup (125ml)
lime juice

1/3 cup (80ml)
fish sauce

1 tablespoon
oyster sauce

2 tablespoons sweet
chilli sauce

2 medium fresh red
chillies, chopped finely

2 teaspoons chopped
fresh lemon grass

2 cloves garlic, crushed

1 tablespoon chopped
fresh mint leaves

1 tablespoon chopped
fresh coriander leaves

1 teaspoon
sambal oelek

1 teaspoon sugar

1/2 teaspoon sesame oil

1 large carrot (180g)

1 large red
capsicum (350g)

125g spinach, shredded

200g snow peas,
shredded

1 1/4 cups (100g)
bean sprouts

Cut squid hoods open, score shallow
criss-cross pattern on inside surface, cut
into 2cm x 7cm pieces.
Cook squid, in batches, in large pan of
boiling water, about 10 seconds or until just
cooked. Rinse under cold water; drain on
absorbent paper.
Shell and devein prawns, cut in half lengthways.
Combine seafood, juice, sauces, chilli, lemon
grass, garlic, herbs, sambal, sugar and oil in
large bowl. Cover; refrigerate 2 hours.
Cut carrot and capsicum into thin 7cm strips,
combine in bowl with spinach, snow peas
and sprouts.
Just before serving, gently combine vegetable
mixture with undrained marinated seafood.

coconut prawn pancakes
with spicy salsa

150g cooked crab meat

1/3 cup (50g)
self-raising flour

1/3 cup (80ml)
coconut milk

2 tablespoons milk

1 egg yolk

2 teaspoons fish sauce

1 1/2 teaspoons green
curry paste (see page 32)

500g large uncooked
prawns, shelled,
chopped finely

1/4 cup (60ml) peanut oil

spicy salsa

1 medium mango (430g),
chopped finely

3 large egg tomatoes
(270g), seeded,
chopped finely

1 green onion,
chopped finely

1 tablespoon sweet
chilli sauce

2 teaspoons
balsamic vinegar

2 teaspoons lime juice

2 tablespoons chopped
fresh coriander leaves

Squeeze excess moisture from crab. Place flour in medium bowl, gradually stir in combined milks, egg yolk, sauce and paste; beat until smooth. Stir in crab and prawns.

Heat oil in large frying pan, drop rounded tablespoons of prawn mixture into pan; spread to 7cm rounds. Cook until bubbles appear, turn pancakes, cook until browned on other side and cooked through. Cover pancakes to keep warm. You will need 12 pancakes for this recipe. Just before serving, top pancakes with Spicy Salsa.

Spicy Salsa Combine ingredients in medium bowl.

prawn and lime

noodle salad

200g dried
rice noodles

800g medium
cooked prawns

200g snow peas,
sliced thinly

250g yellow teardrop
tomatoes, halved

8 green onions,
sliced thinly

1 large red capsicum
(350g), sliced thinly

1/2 cup fresh
coriander leaves

dressing

1 tablespoon finely
chopped fresh
lemon grass

1/4 cup (60ml) sweet
chilli sauce

1/4 cup (60ml)
lime juice

1/4 cup (60ml)
rice vinegar

Place noodles in large heatproof bowl,
cover with boiling water, stand only until just
tender; drain.

Shell and devein prawns, leaving tails intact.

Combine noodles, prawns, snow peas, tomato,
onion, capsicum, coriander and Dressing in
large bowl.

Dressing Combine ingredients in jar; shake well.

50 crispy fried
noodles (mee krob)

vegetable oil, for deep-frying
125g rice vermicelli noodles
1¹/₂ tablespoons peanut oil
2 eggs, beaten lightly
1 tablespoon water
500g minced chicken
¹/₄ cup (60ml) lemon juice
2 tablespoons fish sauce
2 tablespoons tomato sauce
1 teaspoon soy sauce
2 tablespoons brown sugar
1 birdseye chilli, chopped finely
1 tablespoon finely chopped fresh coriander leaves
3 green onions, sliced finely
300g firm tofu, chopped coarsely

Heat vegetable oil in large saucepan; deep-fry noodles, in batches, until puffed. Drain noodles on absorbent paper.
Heat 1 teaspoon of the peanut oil in wok or large pan; pour in ¹/₂ of the combined egg and water. Swirl heated wok to make a thin omelette; cook until just set. Transfer omelette to chopping board, roll tightly; cut into thin strips. Repeat with 1 more teaspoon of the peanut oil and remaining egg mixture.
Heat remaining peanut oil in same wok; stir-fry chicken until browned and cooked through. Add combined juice, sauces, sugar, chilli and coriander; stir-fry 1 minute. Add onion, tofu and omelette strips; stir-fry until heated through. Just before serving, gently toss noodles through chicken mixture.

52 lamb with baby corn

and snow pea sprouts

1 tablespoon peanut oil

700g lamb eye of loin, sliced thinly

100g fresh baby corn, sliced

100g snow peas, sliced

4 green onions, sliced finely

1/2 cup (125ml) sweet chilli sauce

1 tablespoon fish sauce

2 tablespoons lime juice

1 cup (55g) snow pea sprouts

1/2 cup (75g) coarsely chopped unsalted roasted peanuts

Heat oil in wok or large frying pan; stir-fry lamb, in batches, until browned. Stir-fry corn, snow peas and onion in same wok, until tender.
Return lamb to wok with combined sauces and juice; stir-fry until sauce boils. Add sprouts and peanuts; stir-fry, tossing until combined.

satay beef

noodles

2 tablespoons
peanut oil

750g beef rump steak,
sliced thinly

1 medium brown onion
(150g), sliced finely

1 clove garlic, crushed

1/2 cup (130g) smooth
peanut butter

1/4 cup (60ml) sweet
chilli sauce

2/3 cup (160ml)
coconut milk

3/4 cup (180ml)
chicken stock

2 tablespoons
lime juice

1 teaspoon sugar

1 tablespoon finely
chopped fresh
coriander leaves

450g fresh chow
mein noodles

50g garlic chives,
halved lengthways

Heat 1/2 of the oil in wok or large frying pan;
stir-fry beef, in batches, until browned and
almost cooked. Cover to keep warm.
Heat remaining oil in same wok; stir-fry onion
and garlic until onion is soft. Add peanut
butter, sauce, milk, stock, juice, sugar and
coriander; stir-fry until heated through.
Meanwhile, rinse noodles in hot water
to separate; drain.
Return beef and any juices to wok. Gently
toss chives and noodles with beef; stir-fry
until just heated through.

54 green
chicken curry

750g chicken thigh fillets
250g green beans
$1/4$ cup green curry paste (see page 32)
400ml coconut cream

Cut chicken into thin strips. Cut beans into 5cm pieces.
Heat wok or large frying pan, add green curry paste; cook, stirring, about 3 minutes or until fragrant.
Add chicken; cook, stirring, about 10 minutes or until chicken is almost cooked. Stir in coconut cream, bring to boil; simmer, uncovered, 30 minutes. Add beans; simmer 10 minutes or until just tender.

lamb coriander salad

2 tablespoons
peanut oil

750g lamb fillets

2 medium
carrots (240g)

300g curly endive

1/4 cup (35g) coarsely
chopped unsalted
roasted cashews

marinade

1/3 cup coarsely
chopped fresh
coriander leaves

1/3 cup (80ml)
lemon juice

2 tablespoons
fish sauce

1 teaspoon
sambal oelek

1 tablespoon crunchy
peanut butter

Heat oil in large frying pan; cook lamb until browned all over and cooked
as desired, slice lamb. Combine lamb with Marinade in large bowl.
Cover; refrigerate 3 hours or overnight.
Using a vegetable peeler, cut carrot into thin strips. Serve lamb
mixture and carrot strips on endive leaves; sprinkle with nuts.
Marinade Combine ingredients in small bowl.

thai-style **fried** rice

You will need approximately ⅔ cup (130g) of uncooked jasmine rice.

1 tablespoon peanut oil

2 cloves garlic, crushed

1 teaspoon grated
fresh ginger

2 teaspoons chopped
fresh lemon grass

250g minced pork

1 trimmed (75g) celery
stick, sliced finely

1 large red capsicum
(350g), chopped finely

1 medium carrot (120g),
chopped finely

6 green onions,
chopped finely

1 cup (125g)
frozen peas

2 cups cooked
jasmine rice

440g can pineapple
pieces in natural
juice, drained

2 tablespoons chopped
fresh basil leaves

2 teaspoons brown sugar

¼ cup (60ml) lime juice

1 tablespoon soy sauce

1 teaspoon fish sauce

¼ cup finely chopped
fresh coriander leaves

¼ cup (35g) coarsely
chopped unsalted
roasted peanuts

Heat oil in wok or large frying pan; stir-fry garlic,
ginger, lemon grass and pork until pork is
browned. Add celery, capsicum, carrot, onion
and peas; stir-fry until vegetables are tender.
Add rice, pineapple, basil, sugar, juice
and sauces; stir-fry until heated through.
Serve sprinkled with coriander and nuts.

58 thai-style chickpea
and noodle salad

150g rice vermicelli
noodles

500g broccoli,
cut into florets

500g snow peas

3 medium
carrots (360g)

2 x 300g cans
chickpeas,
rinsed, drained

2 tablespoons finely
chopped fresh
coriander leaves

dressing

1/2 cup (125ml)
lime juice

1/4 cup (50g)
brown sugar

2 stems fresh lemon
grass, sliced thinly

1 teaspoon
sambal oelek

Place noodles in large heatproof bowl, cover with boiling water, stand
only until just tender; drain.

Boil, steam or microwave broccoli and snow peas, separately, until just
tender; cool. Cut carrots into thin strips. Combine broccoli, snow peas,
carrot, noodles, chickpeas and coriander in large bowl; mix well. Just
before serving, drizzle with Dressing; toss gently.

Dressing Combine ingredients in jar; shake well.

1 tablespoon
peanut oil

2 birdseye chillies,
chopped finely

1 clove garlic, crushed

2 teaspoons grated
fresh ginger

1 medium brown onion
(150g), sliced finely

500g lamb
fillets, sliced

1 tablespoon
fish sauce

2 teaspoons sugar

3/4 cup (180ml)
coconut cream

2 tablespoons finely
chopped fresh
coriander leaves

Heat oil in wok or large frying pan; stir-fry chilli, garlic, ginger and onion, until onion is soft. Remove from wok.

Stir-fry lamb, in batches, in same wok, until browned all over and cooked as desired.

Return onion mixture to wok with lamb and remaining ingredients; stir-fry, tossing until hot.

glossary

beef

rump steak: boneless tender cut.

strips: prepared from blade, fillet, rib-eye, round, rump, sirloin and topside.

bok choy also called pak choi or Chinese white cabbage; has a fresh, mild mustard taste. Baby bok choy is more tender.

breadcrumbs

stale: one- or two-day-old bread made into crumbs by grating, blending or processing.

capsicum also known as bell pepper or, simply, pepper.

chickpeas also called garbanzos.

chillies see Thai Essential Ingredients, page 3.

choy sum also known as flowering bok choy or flowering white cabbage.

coconut

cream: available in cans and cartons; made from coconut and water.

milk: pure, unsweetened coconut milk in cans.

coriander see Thai Essential Ingredients, page 3.

curry paste commercial versions are available, or see pages 32 to 33 to make your own red, green or massaman curry pastes.

curry powder a blend of the following ground spices: dried chilli, cinnamon, mace, coriander, cumin, fennel, fenugreek, cardamom and turmeric.

eggplant, Thai also called Oriental eggplant; has small, round shape.

eggs some recipes call for raw or barely cooked eggs; exercise caution if there is a salmonella problem in your area.

endive a curly leafed vegetable, mainly used in salads.

fish sauce see Thai Essential Ingredients, page 2.

flour

white plain: an all-purpose flour, made from wheat.

garam masala a blend of spices, originating in North India; based on cardamom, cinnamon, cloves, fennel, coriander and cumin, roasted and ground together. Black pepper and chilli can be added for a hotter version.

garlic chives flat-leafed with stronger flavour than chives.

kaffir lime leaves see Thai Essential Ingredients, page 3.

lemon grass see Thai Essential Ingredients, page 2.

mushrooms

dried shiitake: have a meaty flavour; sold dried, soak to rehydrate before use.

straw: Chinese mushroom with earthy flavour; sold canned in brine.

noodles

bean thread vermicelli: also called cellophane noodles.

dried rice noodles: made from rice flour and water.

Hokkien: also known as stir-fry noodles; fresh wheat-flour noodles.

rice vermicelli: thin, clear rice noodles.

thin dried wheat: long, thin wheat-flour noodles.

oil

peanut: from ground peanuts; has high smoke point.

sesame: made from white sesame seeds; a flavouring rather than cooking medium.

vegetable: any of a number of oils sourced from plants rather than animal fats.

onion

green: also known as scallion or (incorrectly) shallot; an immature onion having a long, green edible stalk.

red: also known as Spanish, red Spanish or Bermuda onion; a sweet-flavoured, large, purple-red onion.

oyster sauce Asian sauce made from oysters and their brine, salt and soy sauce; thickened with starches.

rice vinegar made from fermented rice; colourless and flavoured with sugar and salt. Also known as Seasoned Rice Vinegar.

sambal oelek (also ulek or olek) Indonesian paste made from ground chillies, sugar and spices.

snake beans long, thin, round green beans; Asian in origin.

snow peas also called mange tout ("eat all").

spatchcock a small chicken (poussin), no more than 6 weeks old, weighing a maximum 500g.

star anise dried star-shaped pod whose seeds have an astringent aniseed flavour.

sugar we used granulated table sugar, also known as crystal sugar, unless otherwise specified.

brown: a soft, fine granulated sugar retaining molasses for its colour and flavour.

palm: see Thai Essential Ingredients, page 2.

raw: natural brown granulated sugar.

sweet chilli sauce mild, Thai-type sauce of red chillies, sugar, garlic and vinegar.

tamarind

sauce: if unavailable, soak about 30g dried tamarind in 1 cup of hot water, stand 10 minutes, squeeze pulp as dry as possible and use the flavoured water.

thick concentrate: a thick, purple-black, ready-to-use paste extracted from the pulp of the tamarind bean.

teriyaki sauce a sauce usually made from soy sauce, mirin, sugar, ginger and other spices.

tofu also known as bean curd, an off-white, custard-like product made from the "milk" of crushed soy beans; comes fresh as soft or firm, and processed as fried or pressed dried sheets.

Leftover fresh tofu can be refrigerated in water (which is changed daily) up to 4 days. Silken tofu refers to the method by which it is made, where it is strained through silk.

tomato

paste: a concentrated tomato puree used to flavour soups, stews, sauces and casseroles.

sauce: also known as ketchup or catsup; a flavoured condiment made from tomatoes, vinegar and spices.

teardrop: small, yellow pear-shaped tomatoes.

water chestnuts small, brown tubers with crisp, nutty-tasting flesh. Their crunchy texture is best when fresh, but canned water chestnuts are easily obtained and will keep about a month, once opened, in the refrigerator.

zucchini also known as courgette.

index

facts and figures 63

These conversions are approximate only, but the difference between an exact and the approximate conversion of various liquid and dry measures is minimal and will not affect your cooking results.

Note: NZ, Canada, USA and UK all use 15ml tablespoons. Australian tablespoons measure 20ml.
All cup and spoon measurements are level.

Measuring equipment

The difference between one country's measuring cups and another's is, at most, within a 2 or 3 teaspoon variance. (For the record, 1 Australian metric measuring cup holds approximately 250ml.) The most accurate way of measuring dry ingredients is to weigh them. For liquids, use a clear glass or plastic jug having metric markings.

How to measure

When using graduated measuring cups, shake dry ingredients loosely into the appropriate cup. Do not tap the cup on a bench or tightly pack the ingredients unless directed to do so. Level the top of measuring cups and measuring spoons with a knife. When measuring liquids, place a clear glass or plastic jug having metric markings on a flat surface to check accuracy at eye level.

Dry Measures

metric	imperial
15g	1/2oz
30g	1oz
60g	2oz
90g	3oz
125g	4oz (1/4lb)
155g	5oz
185g	6oz
220g	7oz
250g	8oz (1/2lb)
280g	9oz
315g	10oz
345g	11oz
375g	12oz (3/4lb)
410g	13oz
440g	14oz
470g	15oz
500g	16oz (1lb)
750g	24oz (1 1/2lb)
1kg	32oz (2lb)

We use large eggs having an average weight of 60g.

Liquid Measures

metric	imperial
30ml	1 fluid oz
60ml	2 fluid oz
100ml	3 fluid oz
125ml	4 fluid oz
150ml	5 fluid oz (1/4 pint/1 gill)
190ml	6 fluid oz
250ml (1cup)	8 fluid oz
300ml	10 fluid oz (1/2 pint)
500ml	16 fluid oz
600ml	20 fluid oz (1 pint)
1000ml (1litre)	1 3/4 pints

Helpful Measures

metric	imperial
3mm	1/8in
6mm	1/4in
1cm	1/2in
2cm	3/4in
2.5cm	1in
6cm	2 1/2in
8cm	3in
20cm	8in
23cm	9in
25cm	10in
30cm	12in (1ft)

Oven Temperatures

These oven temperatures are only a guide. Always check the manufacturer's manual.

	°C (Celsius)	°F (Fahrenheit)	Gas Mark
Very slow	120	250	1
Slow	150	300	2
Moderately slow	160	325	3
Moderate	180 –190	350 – 375	4
Moderately hot	200 – 210	400 – 425	5
Hot	220 – 230	450 – 475	6
Very hot	240 – 250	500 – 525	7

at your fingertips

These elegant slipcovers store up to 10 mini books and make the books instantly accessible.

And the metric measuring cups and spoons make following our recipes a piece of cake.

Book Holder
Australia and overseas:
$A8.95 (incl. GST).

Metric Measuring Set
Australia: $6.50 (incl. GST).
New Zealand: $A8.00.
Elsewhere: $A9.95.
Prices include postage and handling.
This offer is available in all countries.

Mail or fax Photocopy and complete the coupon below and post to AWW Home Library Reader Offer, ACP Direct, PO Box 7036, Sydney NSW 1028, or fax to (02) 9267 4363.

Phone Have your credit card details ready, then, if you live in Sydney, phone 9260 0000; if you live elsewhere in Australia, phone 1800 252 515 (free call, Mon-Fri, 8.30am - 5.30pm).

Australian residents We accept the credit cards listed on the coupon, money orders and cheques.

Overseas residents We accept the credit cards listed on the coupon, drafts in $A drawn on an Australian bank, and also British, New Zealand and U.S. cheques in the currency of the country of issue.

Photocopy and complete the coupon below

- -

☐ **Book holder**   ☐ **Metric measuring set**
Please indicate number(s) required.

Mr/Mrs/Ms _____

Address _____

_____

Postcode _____ Country _____

Phone: Business hours ( ) _____

I enclose my cheque/money order for $_____ payable to ACP Direct

OR: please charge $ _____ to my: ☐ Bankcard   ☐ Visa

☐ Amex   ☐ MasterCard   ☐ Diners Club   Expiry Date ___/___

Cardholder's signature _____

Please allow up to 30 days for delivery within Australia.
Allow up to 6 weeks for overseas deliveries. Both offers expire 31/12/02.
HLMI02.

Food editor Pamela Clark
Associate food editor Karen Hammial
Assistant food editor Kathy McGarry
Assistant recipe editor Elizabeth Hooper

HOME LIBRARY STAFF
Editor-in-chief Susan Tomnay
Editor Julie Collard
Concept design Jackie Richards
Designer Mary Keep
Book sales manager Jennifer McDonald
Production manager Carol Currie
Group publisher Jill Baker
Publisher Sue Wannan
Chief executive officer John Alexander

Produced by The Australian Women's Weekly Home Library, Sydney.

Colour separations by ACP Colour Graphics Pty Ltd, Sydney.
Printing by Dai Nippon Printing in Hong Kong

Published by ACP Publishing Pty Limited, 54 Park St, Sydney; GPO Box 4088, Sydney, NSW 1028. Ph: (02) 9282 8618 Fax: (02) 9267 9438.

awwhomelib@acp.com.au
www.awwbooks.com.au

Australia Distributed by Network Distribution Company, GPO Box 4088, Sydney, NSW 1028. Ph: (02) 9282 8777 Fax: (02) 9264 3278.

United Kingdom Distributed by Australian Consolidated Press (UK), Moulton Park Business Centre, Red House Road, Moulton Park, Northampton, NN3 6AQ. Ph: (01604) 497 531 Fax: (01604) 497 533 acpukltd@aol.com

Canada Distributed by Whitecap Books Ltd, 351 Lynn Ave, North Vancouver, BC, V7J 2C4, Ph: (604) 980 9852.

New Zealand Distributed by Netlink Distribution Company, Level 4, 23 Hargreaves St, College Hill, Auckland 1, Ph: (9) 302 7616.

South Africa Distributed by:
PSD Promotions (Pty) Ltd, PO Box 1175, Isando 1600, SA, Ph: (011) 392 6065; and CNA Limited, Newsstand Division, PO Box 107 Johannesburg 2000. Ph: (011) 491 7500.

Great cuisines: Thai Cooking.

Includes index.
ISBN 1 86396 174 7

1. Cookery, Thai.
I. Title: Australian Women's Weekly.
(Series: Australian Women's Weekly Great cuisines mini series).
641.59593

© ACP Publishing Pty Limited 2000
ABN 18 053 273 546

First published 2000. Reprinted 2001.

Cover: Thai beef salad, page 9.
Stylist Sarah O'Brien
Photographer Scott Cameron
Back cover: Baked garlic quail, page 18.

The publishers would like to thank:
Made In Japan, Paddington, NSW, and Mrs Red & Sons, Surry Hills, NSW.